The Severan Dynasty: The History and Legacy of the An Empire's Rulers Before Rome's Imperial Crisis

By Charles River Editors

An ancient portrait of Septimius Severus and his family

About Charles River Editors

Charles River Editors provides superior editing and original writing services across the digital publishing industry, with the expertise to create digital content for publishers across a vast range of subject matter. In addition to providing original digital content for third party publishers, we also republish civilization's greatest literary works, bringing them to new generations of readers via ebooks.

Sign up here to receive updates about free books as we publish them, and visit Our Kindle Author Page to browse today's free promotions and our most recently published Kindle titles.

Introduction

The Severan Dynasty

Caracalla and Geta by Lawrence Alma-Tadema (1907)

"From the study of this history we may also learn how a good government is to be established; for while all the emperors who succeeded to the throne by birth, except Titus, were bad, all were good who succeeded by adoption, as in the case of the five from Nerva to Marcus. But as soon as the empire fell once more to the heirs by birth, its ruin recommenced…Titus, Nerva, Trajan, Hadrian, Antoninus, and Marcus had no need of praetorian cohorts, or of countless legions to guard them, but were defended by their own good lives, the good-will of their subjects, and the attachment of the senate." – Niccolo Machiavelli

"If a man were called upon to fix that period in the history of the world during which the condition of the human race was most happy and prosperous he would, without hesitation, name that which elapsed from the deaths of Domitian to the accession of Commodus."[1] – Edward Gibbon

"The Five Good Emperors," a reference to the five emperors who ruled the Roman Empire between 96 and 180 CE (Nerva, Trajan, Hadrian, Antoninus Pius, and Marcus Aurelius), was a

---

[1] Chapter 3, p. 93, *The History of the Decline and Fall of the Roman Empire, Vol. 1* by E. Gibbon (H. Trevor-Roper, ed., 6 volumes 1993-1994). New York: Everyman's Library.

term first coined by Machiavelli[2] and later adopted and popularized by historian Edward Gibbon, who said that under these men, the Roman Empire "was governed by absolute power under the guidance of wisdom and virtue."[3]

This period of 84 years is generally regarded as the high point of the Roman Empire, at least after Augustus, but what is uncertain and a matter of ongoing debate is whether the five emperors were personally responsible for the situation and the accompanying prosperity enjoyed throughout the empire at the time or if they were simply the beneficiaries of the *Pax Romana*, inaugurated by Augustus in the early part of the 1st century CE. In other words, historians have wondered whether anyone in power during those years would have enjoyed the same rewards.

The description of these rulers as "good" is also a matter of interpretation, with some scholars suggesting they were only "good" in comparison to the preceding emperor (Domitian) and the emperor who followed Marcus Aurelius (Commodus). Both of them were horrible rulers in every aspect, making their near contemporaries look all the better.

Regardless, it is clear that the era of the Five Good Emperors was one of unparalleled success and wealth, and the reasons Rome reached its zenith at this time are worthy of scrutiny. Perhaps most noteworthy is that none of these five emperors were blood relatives - while the final two are often referred to as the Antonines, they were not, in fact, related except by adoption, a practice that may in itself provide at least part of the answer to the question as to why this particular period was so magnificent.

These 84 years also witnessed an impressive growth in the size of the Roman Empire. New acquisitions ranged from northern Britain to Arabia, Mesopotamia, and Dacia. Furthermore, existing possessions were consolidated, and the empire's defenses improved when compared to what had come before. A range of countries that had been client states became fully integrated provinces, and even Italy saw administrative reforms which created further wealth. Throughout the empire, the policy of Romanization proved successful, at least in terms of introducing a common language, enabling standards of living to rise, and creating a political system minimizing internal strife.

With all of that said, according to some academics, the success these rulers had in centralizing the empire's administration, while undoubtedly bringing huge benefits, also sowed the seeds for later problems. After all, as so many Roman emperors proved, from Caligula and Nero to Commodus, the empire's approach to governance was predicated on the ruler's ability. When incompetent or insane emperors came to power, the whole edifice came tumbling down.

The Severan dynasty came shortly after the Five Good Emperors, and it also consisted of five

---

[2] Machiavelli *Discourses on Livy*, I. 10.4.
[3] *The History of the Decline and Fall of the Roman Empire* by E. Gibbon (H. Trevor-Roper, ed., 6 volumes 1993-1994). New York: Everyman's Library.

emperors who ruled the empire from 193-235, except for a brief interlude between 217 and 218 when Macrinus held the imperial throne. In chronological order, the five were Septimius Severus the Founder (193-211), Caracalla (198-217), Geta (209-211), Elagabalus (218-221), and Alexander Severus (222-235). Their reigns coincided with the period in Roman history characterized by academics as the "High Point" of the empire,[4] but this specific dynastic period, following the troubled years after the rule of Marcus Aurelius' son Commodus, did not see the empire return to the heights reached under the Five Good Emperors.[5] It was a period in which the inherent weaknesses of the imperial system were exacerbated, and the policies of successive emperors paved the way for the era generally known as Rome's Imperial Crisis or "The Time of Chaos" (235-284).

Septimus would go on to restore order following the brief civil war of the 190s, though the success of the other Severans' ability to hold the empire together should not be underestimated. By the time of Elagabalus and Alexander Severus, imperial authority was in decline, and Rome faced formidable external challenges to its very existence. The Severans, also known as the Septimii, were of Punic African and Italian origin. The family hailed from the equestrian order and had risen steadily so that by the time of the dynasty's birth, the first two members had already become senators and consuls. Septimius was to become the first emperor of North African origin, and he established the dynasty at the helm of the empire in one of its most difficult periods.

The Severans' story encapsulates many highs and lows, including able and venal emperors, expansion and loss of territory, great artistic achievements, and intellectual advancements, coupled with some of the worst cruelty ever perpetrated by Romans. The Severans have also fared well historically thanks to their successors, because the 50 years following the assassination of Severus Alexander on March 19, 235 has been generally regarded by academics as one of the lowest points in the history of the Roman Empire. Severus Alexander was the last of the Severan emperors, and the subsequent years of crisis (235-285) were characterized by a series of short reigns, usually ending in the violent death of the reigning emperor. At the same time, this period of time also saw the empire beset by threatening forces on all sides. The Romans faced a newly resurgent Persia in the east, as well as significant forces from German tribes on the Rhine and Goths along the Danube. The various conflicts would result in the unprecedented death of a sitting emperor in battle, which took place in 251 with Emperor Decius, and Emperor Valerian was also captured in 260.

The Severan Dynasty: The History and Legacy of the Ancient Roman Empire's Rulers Before Rome's Imperial Crisis looks at these emperors' lives and reigns, and how Rome flourished

---

[4] The "High Point of Empire" of the Roman Empire is a generally accepted term covering the years 96 A.D. to 235 A.D. when the Empire was at its greatest in terms of wealth and territory etc.
[5] The "Five Good Emperors" are: Nerva (96-98 A.D.), Trajan (98-117 A.D.), Hadrian (117-138 A.D.), Antoninus Pius (138-161 A.D.), and Marcus Aurelius (161-180 A.D.).

during that time. Along with pictures depicting important people, places, and events, you will learn about the Severan dynasty like never before.

The Severan Dynasty: The History and Legacy of the Ancient Roman Empire's Rulers Before Rome's Imperial Crisis

About Charles River Editors

Introduction

    Septimius Severus and the Start of the Severan Dynasty

    Caracalla and Geta

    Macrinus and Diadumenianus

    Elagabalus

    Alexander Severus

    The Severan Princesses

    The Aftermath and Legacy of the Severan Dynasty

    Online Resources

    Further Reading

Free Books by Charles River Editors

Discounted Books by Charles River Editors

Septimius Severus and the Start of the Severan Dynasty

Marcus Aurelius, the last of the Five Good Emperors, faced numerous threats across the Roman Empire when he returned to Rome in 176 CE, planning once again to end the ongoing problems along the Danube frontier. He took his son, Commodus, with him on this campaign, and by 179, the Marcomanni had been crushed to the point that they were virtually extinct. He intended to carry out what today would be called ethnic cleansing so that the area east of the Danube could be settled and become a Roman province. Trajan, too, had dreamed of creating a new province in the region, and like him, Marcus Aurelius would not succeed. In 180, Marcus Aurelius fell ill and handed power over to his son before dying shortly thereafter.

Those campaigns were not the only difficulties Marcus Aurelius had to face during his reign. The wars were ruinously expensive, and the sound financial practices of his predecessors, though enabling him to finance the conflicts, did not provide a bottomless money pit. Revenues dropped, and in 169 CE, Marcus Aurelius resorted to auctioning imperial property off to pay his troops. Desperate for money, he took more and more control away from local administrators, thus consolidating and increasing the degree of centralization initiated by his predecessors.

The financial concerns also meant that unlike his immediate predecessors, Marcus Aurelius was never in a position to embark on major building projects. The two best known projects are both memorials to his campaigns: the Aurelian Column and a triumphal arch. The column was 100 Roman feet in height, contained a spiraling relief depicting events during his Danube campaigns. It was quite obviously modeled on Trajan's Column, a gift from the Senate that stood outside the temple dedicated to him. The arch has completely disappeared, though some of the panels decorating it were re-used on the Arch of Constantine.

There are very few physical remains that demonstrate Marcus Aurelius' impact on Rome and his legacy. One of the reasons Marcus Aurelius is considered a truly great emperor is due to writings of his that survived. He was a Stoic, and much of his philosophy was passed down in a 12-book record of his reflections, confessions, and warnings. The books were entitled *To Myself*, but they are now known as the *Meditations*. They were written in the later years of his life while on campaign on the Danube. It has been suggested that he wrote them to console himself during the long years of privation he endured while prosecuting the war.

His core belief was in the principle of virtue through duty to oneself and others. Much of his writing is quite dark, and he repeatedly reflects on the nearness of death and the transitory nature of human existence.

His thoughts, on the other hand, confirm that he was a genuine thinker and a true philosopher king. He wrote, "The first rule is to keep an untroubled spirit, for all things must bow to Nature's law and soon enough you must vanish into nothingness, like Hadrian and Augustus. The second is to look things in the face and know them for what they are remembering that it is your duty to be a good man. Do without flinching what man's nature demands, say what seems to you most just though with courtesy modesty and sincerity."[6]

The *Historia Augusta* described Marcus Aurelius as "a solemn child from the very beginning and as soon as he passed beyond the age when children are brought up under the care of nurses, he was handed over to advanced instructors and attained to a knowledge of philosophy… He studied philosophy with ardour even as a youth. For when he was twelve years old he adopted the dress and a little later the hardiness of a philosopher, pursuing his studies clad in a rough Greek cloak and sleeping on the ground. [A]t his mother's solicitation however, he reluctantly consented to sleep on a couch strewn with skins.[7]

On the basis of this information, it does not seem likely that he enjoyed a fun and frivolous childhood, and his upbringing undoubtedly shaped his later life, especially his fascination with philosophy. Clearly, that philosophy proved so important in shaping his decisions.

---

[6] Marcus Aurelius, *Meditations,* VIII.5.
[7] *Historia Augusta,* Life of Marcus II.1.

A bust of Marcus Aurelius as a young boy

Marcus Aurelius was not the most optimistic of men. Some might say he was simply pragmatic and honest about life, but his attitude was certainly quite depressing. In *Meditations*, he wrote, "Consider for the sake of argument the times of Vespasian. You will see all the same things, men marrying, begetting children, being ill, dying, fighting wars, feasting, trading, farming, flattering, asserting themselves, suspecting, praying for the death of others, grumbling at their present lot, coveting a consulate, coveting a kingdom. Then turn to the times of Trajan, again everything is the same and that life too is dead."[8]

Despite his pessimism, it can be said that, on a personal level, Marcus Aurelius was a good man who defended the territory of the empire in an exemplary fashion. However, if one of the

---

[8] Marcus Aurelius, *Meditations,* IV.32.

main criteria used to determine the success of an emperor is the successor he chooses, then Marcus Aurelius failed spectacularly. He was the first emperor since Vespasian, who had ruled about 100 years before, to leave his son as his successor, and the alacrity with which Marcus Aurelius abandoned the principle of adoption suggests that traditional family ties would have exerted an influence on the choice of emperor sooner if his predecessors had sons to whom the throne could be passed.

Commodus stands alongside Caligula as one of the Roman emperors who contemporaries considered absolutely vile. Commodus became notorious for his paranoia, murdering anyone he suspected of conspiracy and ruling like an absolute dictator way out of his depth. While Marcus Aurelius struggled with depleted funds, Commodus used them to pay his own appearance fees as a gladiator, during which he won fixed matches against real gladiators or beat to death physically disabled individuals and amputees who had been rounded up and tethered together for the spectacle. Commodus also killed all kinds of animals in the arena, and on one occasion beheaded an ostrich and carried it over to the gallery holding various Roman Senators, implicitly threatening to do the same to them.

In the final years, Commodus took things to new heights by renaming the city of Rome to *Colonia Lucia Annia Commodiana*, renaming the months of the year after himself, and depicting himself as a god of herculean strength. The zaniness ended with the assassination of Commodus in 192, which spelled the end of the Nerva–Antonine dynasty and led to civil wars that made 193 the "Year of the Five Emperors," much the same way Nero's death touched off the "Year of the Four Emperors" over 100 years earlier.

Cassius Dio wrote that Commodus was "not naturally wicked but, on the contrary, as guileless as any man that ever lived. His great simplicity, however, together with his cowardice, made him the slave of his companions, and it was through them that he at first, out of ignorance, missed the better life and then was led on into lustful and cruel habits, which soon became second nature."

A bust depicting Commodus as Hercules

In general, despite the one very glaring failure that Commodus represented, Marcus Aurelius ruled with scrupulous care. He was a rigid conservative, especially when it came to maintaining the existing social order, but he was lenient in his rulings and displayed a humanity nearly above reproach. He has often been described as cold and joyless, but his overriding motivation was duty, and in the performance of his duty as he viewed it, he excelled.

The reigns of the Five Good Emperors were undoubtedly the high point of the Roman Empire, which its greatest extent territorially and enjoyed a degree of prosperity and (relative) political tranquility unmatched in any other period of similar length. The fact that they all played their parts in reforms, rebuilt and carried out new construction, and promoted policies which saw the further integration and Romanization of the numerous races within the empire's boundaries is to their collective credit. The five rulers had very different personalities, and it can be argued that the complementary nature of their skills played a part in maintaining this prolonged period of success. Another factor was that they were all chosen to succeed to the throne, rather than having inherited it by dint of direct descent from the previous emperor or seizing power through brute force or subterfuge. This gave them a legitimacy that, when coupled with their natural talents, enabled them to make their own contributions to the empire, and significant ones at that.

Whether the use of the term "good" is appropriate in the characterization of these individuals matters far less than the fact that each ruled in a way that resulted in a positive outcome for the empire. The one negative aspect of their reigns stems from their authoritarian, centralizing tendencies, because no matter how well-intentioned or effective that form of government was in their hands, it paved the way for future problems. That greater degree of centralization worked well in the hands of someone like Marcus Aurelius, but it was utterly disastrous just a few years later when wielded by Commodus.

In the 19th century, Matthew Arnold concluded that the Five Good Emperors "lived and acted in a state of society modern by its essential characteristics, in an epoch akin to our own in a brilliant centre of civilisation."[9] Even though modern historians are now more aware of the inherent weaknesses in the Roman Empire at this time, it is still fair to conclude that these five emperors deserve the epithet that has marked their legacies for centuries.

However, the death of Commodus in 192 plunged the empire into disarray and brought Pertinax, one of the most fascinating, if short-lived, of the Roman emperors, to the throne. Despite holding the imperial crown for only three months, it was his murder and the subsequent civil war that resulted in the emergence of the Severan dynasty.

Pertinax's story was one of rags to riches. His father was a slave who made a fortune in the wool trade after winning his freedom. Pertinax was given a very traditional education and became a teacher, but at the age of 35, he became so dissuaded by the low pay that he embarked on a military career. He rose quickly to become the commander of a cohort of Gauls in Syria before being promoted to Tribune of the VI Legion stationed at York in Britannia. He continued to rise, was posted to the Danube, and served with distinction under Marcus Aurelius. The emperor made him a senator in recognition of his services, and soon after, he became a consul, quickly followed by being awarded the governorship of Dacia and later Syria. He also found favor with Commodus, who sent him back to Britannia to put a mutiny down. He then became governor of Africa, and finally, in 189, he became urban prefect of Rome.

He was in Rome when news of Commodus's death reached the city on December 31, 192. The Senate offered Pertinax the throne, having judged him the best chance for avoiding widespread civil war. The Praetorians were bribed to accept his nomination, and Pertinax threw himself into the task of repairing the damage done by Commodus.

It is the judgment of history that he tried to do too much too quickly. Cassius Dio summed up

---

[9] M. Arnold, *The Victoria Magazine* 2 (1863).

the problem with Emperor Pertinax: "He failed to comprehend, though a man of wide practical experience, that one cannot with safety reform everything at once and that the restoration of a state, in particular, requires both time and wisdom."[10]

Classical Numismatic Group's picture of a coin depicting Pertinax

Pertinax's fate was effectively sealed by his refusal to rein back proposed reforms that would have seen palace officials lose lucrative opportunities to embezzle vast amounts from state funds, and his determination to curb Praetorian power. Within months of coming to power, the Praetorians attempted to assassinate him, but the coup failed and the ringleaders were executed. Three weeks later, on March 28, troops stormed the palace in which he was staying. He refused to flee and tried to reason with them, but to no avail. The 66-year-old was hacked to death, having reigned for only 87 days. The rebellious troops stuck his head on a spear and paraded it around the city on their way back to the Praetorian camp.

This made very clear who the power brokers were in the city, and candidates for the throne rushed to the camp to bid for Praetorian support in their claim to the throne. The Praetorians also realized they had a unique opportunity and thus posted a herald to announce that the throne was effectively "up for auction". Eventually, the choice came down Pertinax's father-in-law, Titus Flavius Sulpicianus, and Didius Julianus. The latter was successful, as he'd made the higher bid, and the Guard was concerned that Titus might harbor a grudge against them for killing his daughter's husband.

Didius Julianus had a very different background than Pertinax. He was brought up in the house of Marcus Aurelius' mother, Domitia Lucillia, and his family was from Milan and well-connected. With the advantage of being a member of the aristocracy, he rose quickly in the army

---

[10] Cassius Dio, *Roman History*, LXXIV.10.

and became commander of the XXII Legion stationed in Germany in 172. He served as consul alongside Pertinax in 175 and was governor of four provinces between the years 172 and 190. When Pertinax was murdered, he was a well-respected senior senator and positioned to secure the throne.

Didius was not without his rivals, and Legions in Syria proclaimed Gaius Pescennius Niger emperor, while Legions in Britain proclaimed Decimus Clodius Albinus. The most significant of all the rival claimants was Septimius Severus, who had the backing of no fewer than 16 Legions on the Danube.

Septimius bought Clodius off by offering him the title of Caesar, and he marched on Rome. Didius did what he could to oppose his progress, including asking the Senate to appoint Septimius as his co-emperor in desperation, but Septimius was already very near Rome and the Senate instead voted to put Didius to death and offer the throne to Septimius. The Senate also decided to deify Pertinax. According to Cassius Dio, Didius Julianus' last words were simple questions: "But what evil have I done? Whom have I killed?"[11] His reign lasted only 66 days, opening a path for Septimius Severus, the first emperor of the Severan dynasty.

---

[11] Cassius Dio, *Roman History*, LXXIV.10.

José Luiz Bernardes Ribeiro's picture of a bust of Didius

Septimius was born in Lepcis Magna on the coast of what is now Libya. It is said he retained his North African accent throughout his life. His father was Publius Septimius Geta, head of an important provincial family. The young Severus was encouraged to embark on the usual route taken by young aristocrats of his class, including marrying relatively early; his first wife was a lady from a respectable family in Lepcis Magna. He travelled to Rome not long after he turned eighteen and rose through the ranks to achieve the governorship of Upper Pannonia in 191 A.D. Aided in his rise by fellow North Africans such as the commander of the Praetorian guard, Aemilius Laetus was well-placed when news reached him of the deaths of Commodus and Pertinax while he was serving in Upper Pannonia.

A bust of Septimius Severus

Septimius was acclaimed emperor by his troops on the Danube and led them to Rome to immediately secure his position. The Senate succumbed without putting up a fight and confirmed him as emperor on June 10, 193, but this accession was marked by a particularly vicious act on the part of the new emperor. Septimius used the pretext that the Praetorians had murdered Pertinax to order the Guard to assemble unarmed outside the city, ostensibly to take part in a parade celebrating his coronation. However, once they had arrived at the designated location, Septimius's men surrounded them and executed the individuals deemed responsible for Pertinax's death. The remainder of the Guard was disbanded and prohibited from coming within 100 miles of Rome. Cruelly, but wisely, the emperor replaced the Guard with troops loyal to himself.

The new emperor's next task was to end the threat posed by Pescennius Niger, who had been proclaimed emperor by his troops in Syria. In 193, Septimius won two major victories against his rival and marched into Syria. The final decisive battle took place in April 194 near where Alexander the Great had won his victory over the Persians on the River Issus. Septimius won an overwhelming victory, and Niger was captured and beheaded without ceremony. Such was the ferocity of Septimius' treatment of his foes that many fled to Parthia rather than risk his wrath. Indeed, Parthia's support for his enemies led him to embark on a campaign against Parthia in 195.

Classical Numismatic Group's picture of a coin depicting Pescennius Niger

No sooner had he defeated his eastern rival than Septimius turned his attention to Decimus Clodius Albinus, another rival in the west. Also of North African descent, Clodius came from an extremely wealthy family. Septimius had initially bought Clodius off by giving him the rank and title of Caesar, but Septimius later changed his mind and had his son, Caracalla, only 7 at the time, proclaimed Caesar. This abruptly let Clodius know that Caracalla was not, in fact, to be

Clodius's successor, as he had assumed. By 196, Clodius decided that he wanted more, and the two fought a civil war. Clodius marched into Gaul, and the two sides fought in February 197 near Lyons. The battle was closely fought, but Septimius eventually emerged victorious and Clodius fled to Lyons, where he was captured and committed suicide. In a typical display of brutality, Septimius lay Codius naked in front of him and rode his horse over his enemy's body. Clodius's head was then cut off and sent to Rome, while his body and those of his entire family were thrown into the River Rhone.

Sailko's picture of a bust of Clodius

Septimius took no chances that there would be further internal opposition to his rule. In 197, he put no fewer than 29 Senators he felt had been supporters of his rivals to death. It was at this time that many started calling him the "Punic Sulla." As this suggests, Septimius never courted popularity with the Senate at any time during his reign, relying instead on the sole support of the army. He took a number of steps to secure the loyalty of the legions, including increasing their pay, improving their daily living conditions, and introducing a variety of reforms, such as allowing troops to marry and live at home rather than in barracks. Septimius was also aware of the need to maintain the loyalty of the Roman masses, which he accomplished by frequently entertaining them with elaborate games and animal shows for their amusement.

The emperor did, however, have serious external threats requiring constant attention. The first of these was the danger posed by Parthia to numerous Roman client-states in the east. His second campaign against the Parthians was a large-scale invasion of Mesopotamia which culminated in a march to Ctesiphon, the Parthian capital.

Once again, Septimius demonstrated his savagery when dealing with his enemies. After capturing the city, all of the men were butchered and the women and children - over 100,000 in number – were sold into slavery. Septimius also took the opportunity to fill his depleted coffers by plundering the Parthian treasury. The northern part of Mesopotamia was taken back under Roman control as it had been in the time of Trajan, and Septimius remained in the east for the next five years, though he was unable to achieve his primary objective: the capture of the city of Harta. Next, he toured Palestine and Egypt, visiting the tomb of Alexander the Great and the great pyramids and temples of Thebes.

Septimius returned to Rome in 202, but by then he was increasingly prone to illness and was, by standards of the time, quite elderly. He was a firm believer in astrology and believed that he had learned of the time of his death through divination. According to Cassius Dio, "He knew this chiefly from the stars under which he had been born, for he had caused them to be painted on the ceilings of the rooms of the palace where he was wont to hold court so that they were visible to all with the exception of the portion which, as the astrologers express it, observed the hour when he first saw the light for this portion he had not depicted in the same way in both rooms."[12]

Septimius's thoughts turned to succession. Caracalla had already been proclaimed Caesar, and Septimius now set about finding a suitable wife for his son. His choice was Publia Fulvia Plautilla, the daughter of his old friend, Commander of the Praetorian Guard Gaius Fulvius.[13] Despite this friendship, Herodian recorded that Plautianus was disliked by most who met him because "he misused his power to commit all kinds of acts of cruelty and violence in everything he did making himself one of the most feared prefects of all time." He allegedly even had those guarding his daughter castrated to ensure that there would be no risk to her virtue.[14]

Caracalla was not happy with his father's choice, and he refused to eat with her or consummate the marriage. He also let both his wife and his father-in-law know that when he came to power, his first act would be to have both of them put to death. The situation came to a head in 202, when Caracalla persuaded three centurions to tell Septimius that Plautianus had ordered them to kill him and Caracalla. Never one to take risks with his life, Septimius had Plautianus executed and his daughter sent into exile on the island of Lipari. When Caracalla came to power, he had his wife murdered, carrying out his previous threat.[15]

---

[12] Cassius Dio, *Roman History*, LXXVII. 11
[13] Herodian, *History of the Empire from the time of Marcus Aurelius,* III.X.
[14] Herodian, *History of the Empire from the time of Marcus Aurelius,* III.X.

Septimius's last years were not without trials. Caracalla and his brother, Publius Septimius Geta, were fierce rivals long before their father's death, and their antagonism only grew as the old emperor's health declined. The two sons and their supporters constantly found ways to irritate the other, so much so that when Septimius embarked on what would be his last campaign after trouble erupted in Britannia, he did not trust either of his sons enough to leave them in Rome. Instead, he insisted they both accompany him.

The journey to Britannia began in early 208, and Septimius suffered so severely from gout that he had to be carried in a litter. Despite his obvious discomfort, he made good progress across Gaul and landed safely in Britannia, determined to settle the issues there once and for all by conquering the whole island. Geta was put in charge of the administration of the empire while Septimius and Caracalla concentrated on the invasion of Scotland. The Romans had limited successes in their campaigns in 209 and 210, and the emperor was increasingly incapacitated by his illness, preventing him from personally directing the campaigns. Caracalla was distinctly uninterested in the venture, and Herodian suggests that the only saving grace, as far as Caracalla was concerned, was the opportunity for him to win favor amongst the troops. Herodian also thought that he was impatient for his father's demise, writing, "He regarded his father, who was suffering from a drawn out illness and taking a long time to die, as a troublesome nuisance and tried to persuade his doctors and attendants to do him some mischief while they tended the old man, so as to get rid of him sooner."[16]

Septimius finally died on February 4, 211 at the age of 65, leaving the conquest of Scotland unfinished. His sons abandoned the campaign and hurried back to Rome, ostensibly to take their father's ashes to be interred in the Mausoleum of Hadrian. The Senate immediately declared Septimius a god, and Herodian summed up his achievements as follows: "No one had ever before been so successful in civil wars, against rivals or in foreign wars against the barbarians. For eighteen years he ruled before making way for his young sons to succeed, bequeathing to them greater wealth than any previous emperor, and an invincible army."[17]

Septimius's achievements were not just in the fields of ensuring economic prosperity and winning military victories. He also left a legacy in terms of the buildings he had built or renovated, even if Cassius Dio was particularly unimpressed in the way he carried out his projects: "He restored a very large number of the ancient buildings and inscribed on them his own name, just as if he had erected them in the first place from his own private funds. He also spent a great deal uselessly in repairing other buildings and in constructing new ones; for instance, he built a temple of huge size to Bacchus and Hercules."[18] Cassius Dio's assessment is a little harsh, given that Septimius had to meet challenges caused by a major fire in 191 that

---

[15] Herodian, *History of the Empire from the time of Marcus Aurelius,* III.X, XIII
[16] Herodian, *History of the Empire from the time of Marcus Aurelius,* III.XV.
[17] Herodian, *History of the Empire from the time of Marcus Aurelius,* III.XV.
[18] Cassius Dio, *Roman History*, LXXVII.16.

resulted in the emperor commissioning a large-scale map of the city, carved on 151 marble slabs and affixed to a wall near Vespasian's Library of Peace.

As others had done before him, Septimius used new buildings as part of a policy to develop the image of his regime. Some of his most ambitious projects have been lost, including the Septizonium, a huge colonnaded façade fronting one corner of the Palatine Hill. He also extended the imperial palace, the remains of which are still visible today.

A 19th century depiction of remains of the Septizonium

The most famous of his monuments was the temple referenced by Cassius Dio in Leptis

Magna, one of many new public buildings he funded in the city of his birth in North Africa. He also built an artificial harbor, new baths, a forum, basilica, other temples, and colonnaded streets. The works were so extensive that the city became the showpiece of Roman Africa.

The Arch of Septimius Severus in Leptis Magna

Ruins of the Severan Basilica in Leptis Magna

Ruins of the theater in Leptis Magna

Sascha Coachman's picture of the ruins of the forum in Leptis Magna

Septimius undoubtedly left the empire wealthy, militarily strong, and in a better place than he had found it. What he did not do, unfortunately, was ensure his successor was up to the task of maintaining his achievements.

Caracalla and Geta

The future Emperor Caracalla was named Lucius Septimius Bassianus when he was born at Lyon in 188. His father was, at the time, governor of Lugdunensis. In his early years, Caracalla was said to be intelligent and sensitive, though he was fiercely antagonistic when it came to his younger brother, who was born the year after him. *Historia Augusta* described him as follows: "He himself in his boyhood was winsome and clever, respectful to his parents and courteous to his parents' friends, beloved by the people, popular with the Senate and people and well able to further his own interests in winning affection. Never did he seem backward in letters or slow in deeds of kindness, never niggardly in largesse or tardy in forgiving."[19] This apparent paragon underwent something of a transformation over the years because the same source was particularly uncomplimentary about Caracalla as an adult: "His mode of life was evil and he was more brutal even than his cruel father. He was gluttonous in his use of food and addicted to wine,

---
[19] *Historia Augusta*, 'The Life of Antoninus Caracalla', I.3.

hated by his household and detested in every camp save that of the Praetorian Guard, and between him and his father there was no resemblance whatever."[20]

Marie-Lan Nguyen's picture of a bust of Caracalla

---

[20] *Historia Augusta*, 'The Life of Antoninus Caracalla', IX.3.

A bust of Geta

Incredibly damning assessments of Caracalla have been consistent throughout the centuries. In virtually all studies of the emperors, he is cast as one of the very worst, with a predilection for violence and cruelty matched only by a few others. That said, while Caracalla is almost universally criticized by contemporary sources and modern historians, that does not mean he was an ineffective emperor. Though he personally had few good traits, he was quite popular with the army.

Septimius had advised his sons to agree with each other, pay the troops well, and rely on no one but themselves. His injunction to his sons to agree was a forlorn hope, given their overt hostility to one another. They were young at the time of their father's death - Caracalla was 23 and Geta 22 - and it was no surprise that upon his father's death, Caracalla took immediate steps to secure the throne for himself. It is likely this had been Septimius's intention, as he had made his older son Imperator Destinatus and Augustus in 196, while Geta was given only the title of Augustus in 209. However, Caracalla's difficulties in securing the throne for himself lay in the fact that his mother, Julia Domna, supported her younger son's claims for joint imperial status. Caracalla found his ambitions continuously thwarted by Julia's determination to secure equality for Geta.

Sailko's picture of a bust of Julia DOmna

    The concept of having two young emperors who so obviously loathed one another ruling jointly was doomed from the very beginning. Some initial attempts were made to coexist, such as dividing the Imperial Palace in two, but each half of the palace had a separate entrance and the brothers blocked them. They set about trying to win the support of the Senators and anyone they deemed to have influence in the empire's politics. Geta, for example, worked hard to win the support of the educated and literary classes and tended to have better press than his brother. Both fought to have their henchmen appointed to official positions and even backed different factions in the circus games.

    Judicial proceedings were not exempt from their interference, as both tried to secure verdicts favorable to their clients. There was not much between them as rulers, and both were guilty of trying to poison the other. Indeed, Cassius Dio's portrayal of Geta was every bit as unflattering as that of Caracalla in *Historia Augusta*. He claimed Geta was parsimonious with his friends but overindulgent himself in the extreme with respect to the money he spent on his personal jewelry and clothing. As was the case with Caracalla, he may have been a little more pleasant in his early years. Cassius Dio wrote, "As a youth he was handsome, brusque in his manners though not disrespectful, incontinent in love, gluttonous and a lover of food and wine variously spiced."[21]

The attempts to work together proved a swift failure. After only a few months of this intolerable situation, the brothers decided that the only viable option was to split the empire between them. The plan was for Geta to have the Asian provinces with his capital at either Alexandria or Antioch, while Caracalla would have Europe and North Africa. The division might have been a practical solution to an intractable problem, but Julia Domna refused to sanction it, so Caracalla felt the need for decisive action. Geta was consistently well-guarded by his supporters, but it is said that Caracalla took the opportunity to kill his brother when they met with their mother. Their joint reign lasted only 10 months.

Geta did have some powerful supporters, and Caracalla realized that his actions would be avenged unless he took immediate steps to prevent retaliation. He ensured the support and protection of the Praetorian Guard by offering them handsome payments to maintain their loyalty. He told them that he was defending himself because his brother had attacked him, and he repeated this story in the Senate the next day. Even so, Caracalla took no chances with his brother's supporters and systematically set about ridding himself of all of those he could find, including Senators, provincial governors, soldiers, friends, and servants. During the first few months of 212, it is estimated that more than 20,000 of those thought to be Geta's supporters had been executed. There were protests against the severity of Caracalla's actions, but these were also put down with great brutality. One of these victims was Cornificia, the daughter of Marcus Aurelius, who had been witnessed weeping for Geta.

Caracalla never regained the trust of the Senate or the people following his campaign of extermination, but it did not prevent him from trying to eradicate his brother's name. Cassius Dio noted, "Caracalla exhibited his hatred for his dead brother by abolishing observance of his birthday, and he vented his anger upon the stones that had supported his statues and melted down the coinage that displayed his image."[22]

Caracalla would never feel at home again in Rome. In 213, he traveled to the German frontier to consolidate his support amongst the troops stationed there. He went out of his way to be seen as one of them, refusing to ride or travel in a carriage, preferring instead to walk and march alongside the soldiers. He also ate only military rations, grinding his allowance of barley into flour. These gestures, alongside the 50% increase in pay, had the desired effect, and he became

---

[21] Cassius Dio, *Roman History*, L.1.
[22] Cassius Dio, *Roman History*, LXXVIII.12.

popular with the army on the Rhine. His military campaign proved as successful as his public relations one, and the Senate awarded him the title of Germanicus Maximus in recognition of his victories.

In 214, Caracalla campaigned further afield in Dacia, Thrace, and Asia Minor. In his journey through Thrace, Cassius Dio says he was enthralled by tales of Alexander the Great and was determined to emulate the successes of his new hero. Just as Alexander had done, Caracalla began to keep elephants, and he began a persecution of Aristotelean philosophers on the grounds that Aristotle had somehow been involved in Alexander's death. Caracalla began a massive program of commissioning and placing statues of the Macedonian king throughout the empire, and his obsession became so great that he also commissioned portraits displaying Alexander's head amalgamated with his own.

A coin depicting Caracalla as a soldier

The winter of 214-215 was spent in Nicodemia and the summer was spent in Antioch. He arrived in Alexandria as autumn drew near and immediately visited Alexander's tomb upon arrival, leaving his cloak and all of his jewelry as an offering.

While there, his troops were involved in an infamous massacre, the exact cause of which is unknown. It is possible the Alexandrians let him know too vociferously of their disquiet when it came to Geta's murder, but whatever the reason, Caracalla's revenge - through which the young men of the city were rounded up by his troops and slaughtered - was extraordinarily brutal, even for him. The massacre spread quickly to other parts of the city, and thousands lost their lives in what was one of the darkest hours in Caracalla's reign and one of the bleakest episodes in the history of the empire.

The reason the emperor had gone to the east in the first place was to mount an expedition against the Parthians, and following events in Alexandria, Caracalla moved on to Syria and assembled an army comprised of eight legions. At the time, the Parthians were embroiled in a civil war of their own, and Caracalla offered an alliance with Artabanus, one of their two rivals, and even offered to marry his daughter to cement the deal. Caracalla, however, seems to have taken advantage of the trust Artabanus had placed in him and invaded unopposed, ravaging the countryside as he went. Having won this rather ignoble victory, Caracalla retired to Edessa for the winter, intending to resume the campaign in the spring of the following year.

Events back in Rome ensured that Caracalla's plans did not come to fruition. Resentment against the emperor had been growing for some time, details of a plot to overthrow him were leaked, and the information ended up in Julia Domna's possession in Antioch. On April 8, Macrinus and Martialis, the leaders of the conspiracy, accompanied Caracalla from Edessa to Carrhae. The emperor was suffering from a severe stomach issue at the time and stopped to relieve himself. Martialis assassinated him at that point with a single sword thrust before turning and fleeing from the scene, but he was brought down by a javelin thrown by one of the guards. Macrinus pleaded his ignorance of the conspiracy and joined in the lamentation of the emperor's death. Caracalla was cremated, and his ashes were returned to Julia Domna in Antioch, where she died shortly afterward. Their ashes were interred together in the Mausoleum of Hadrian, and they were deified six months later.

Caracalla was only 29 when he was assassinated, and despite his reputation as one of Rome's worst emperors, there were also achievements to his name. He extended Roman citizenship in 212, reformed the empire's currency, and was diligent in his involvement in major lawsuits. The most obvious and lasting physical monuments to his reign are the Baths of Caracalla. *Historia Augusta* is fulsome in its praise of this project: "Among the public works which he left at Rome was the notable Bath named after himself, the *cella solaris* of which so the architects declare cannot be reproduced in the way in which it was built by him. For it is said that the whole vaulting rested on gratings of bronze or copper placed underneath it but such is its size that those who are versed in mechanics declare that it could not have been built in this way."[23]

---

[23] *Historia Augusta*, 'Life of Antoninus Caracalla', IX.

A picture of the baths' ruins

Ethan Doyle White's picture of the ruins

The remains of these baths are one of the most impressive monuments of Imperial Rome, and they were considered a wonder at the time of their building. The artistry that went into the construction of the structure made it a marvel in the ancient world, thanks to its mosaic floors, marble veneers, and painted stucco friezes. The baths were dedicated in 216 and are testament to the fact that for all of his many faults, Caracalla did have artistic taste.

Macrinus and Diadumenianus

Caracalla's assassination left no obvious successor, as he had no children and never named an heir. The empire now waited for someone to declare himself the ruler, and after three days, that is exactly what happened.

The rule of Macrinus and his son, Diadumenianus, whom he made his co-emperor, lasted only a year. It is fair to say that this did not provide the new emperor with either time or opportunity to make any real lasting impression on the empire. Indeed, Macrinus's claim to fame, if he had any at all, lay in the fact that he was the first provincial to become emperor. Cassius Dio wrote of him, "He was a Moor by birth from Caesarea and the son of most obscure parents so that he was very appropriately likened to the ass that was led up to the palace by the spirit; in particular one of his ears had been pierced in accordance with the customs followed by most of the Moors. But his integrity threw even this drawback into the shade. As for his attitude towards law and precedent his knowledge of them was not so accurate as his observance of them was faithful."[24]

---

[24] Cassius Dio, *Roman History*, LXXIX.1.1.

José Luiz Bernardes Ribeiro's picture of a bust of Macrinus

Sailko's picture of a gold coin depicting Diadumenianus

Macrinus was a lawyer by training, but he used his links with Plautianus, the commander of the Praetorians under Septimius Severus, to secure a position in the Guard. He became overall commander under Caracalla in 212, which meant he was in a strong position when Caracalla was assassinated, and he moved quickly to secure his position. He executed potential rivals and replaced key provincial governors with supporters from his class. He quickly fell out with Julia Domna and ordered her to leave Antioch. She refused and starved herself to death rather than accept his instructions.

The Parthians regrouped after Caracalla's death, and in the autumn of 217, Macrinus paid the exorbitant sum of 200 million sesterces to bribe them to go away. Not only did this humiliation diminish him in the eyes of the military and the masses, but it also made it impossible for him to maintain the lavish levels of pay Caracalla had previously provided the troops to maintain their loyalty.

It was during this uneasy period that Varius Avitus, better known as Elagabalus, the 14-year-old great nephew of Julia Domna, was proclaimed emperor on May 15, 218 by the 3rd Legion Gallica. Macrinus's response was to name his 9-year-old son, Diadumenianus, to the position of Augustus, using the occasion to distribute money to the troops in the hope of winning their support. *Historia Augusta* offered a description of Diadumenianus, perhaps the least-known Roman emperor: "The boy himself was beautiful beyond all others, somewhat tall of stature, with golden hair, black eyes, and an aquiline nose; his chin was wholly lovely in its modelling, his mouth designed for a kiss, and he was by nature strong and by training graceful."[25]

Macrinus's tactics failed to win the support for which he had hoped, so he had to flee to Antioch. On June 8, 218, he was defeated in a battle outside the city and tried to escape northward with the intention of reaching Rome to carry on the war against the rebels from there. However, he was captured at the Phosphorous, and in the process of being taken back to Antioch, he was murdered on the way south in Cappadocia. He was 53, and his son, whom he had sent to what he hoped would be safety in Parthia, was also captured and executed at Zeugma.

Elagabalus

Macrinus had apparently failed to learn the lesson that the army was the key to the imperial purple. By reducing their pay and submitting to a humiliating peace with Parthia, he lost all hope of consolidating his position. His successor, Elagabalus, began as emperor with an immediate advantage over his predecessor due to rumors that he was the illegitimate son of Caracalla.

---

[25] *Historia Augusta*, 'Life of Diadumenianus', III.

José Luiz Bernardes Ribeiro's picture of a bust of Elagabalus

If Macrinus and his son made little impression on Rome and the Romans, the same cannot be said for Elagabalus, whose antics shocked even the most jaded of Senators and citizens. According to *Historia Augusta's* "Life of Elagabalus," he was "so detestable for his life, his character and his utter depravity that the Senate expunged from the records even his name."[26] Ancient historians condemned this young Syrian, who was once the Sun God's high priest and whose lifestyle and attempts to elevate the worship of the Sun God were deeply resented by the Roman establishment.

Born Varius Avitus Bassianus, Elagabalus was the grandson of Julia Maesa, the younger sister of Julia Domna. His father was officially Sextus Varius Marcellus, who was made Senator by Caracalla, though his mother maintained that his biological father was, in fact, the emperor.

---

[26] *Historia Augusta,* 'Life of Elagabalus', XVIII.1.

There is no proof that this claim has any validity, but it was believed by a significant number of the troops whose loyalty Caracalla had so assiduously wooed, and this support became crucial in securing the throne for Elagabalus.

Classical Numismatic Group's picture of a coin depicting Julia Maesa

The plot to depose Macrinus was hatched by Gannys, who was Elagabalus's mother's lover at the time. When he was acclaimed emperor, the young ruler took the title of Marcus Aurelius Antoninus, but he quickly proved he was not much like his namesake. Having been raised to the purple, the new emperor spent several months in Antioch and Nicodemia, where he gave some indication of what was to come by having Gannys executed. The young boy clearly was not proving as malleable as those who had put him on the throne had hoped. The death of Gannys, however, gave Elagablus's mother, Julia Soaemis, and his grandmother, Julia Maesa, the opportunity to become the real power behind the throne. They quickly realized that they could keep Elagabalus occupied by encouraging and assisting his excesses while they got on with the governing of the empire.

Wolfgang Sauber's picture of a sculpture of Julia Soaemis

When Elagabalus arrived in Rome in 219 along his retinue of Syrian family members and acolytes, he brought with him the black stone that played a prominent part in the cult of Elagabalus, the Sun God, which had been set up in the temple at Emesa. Herodian described it as being "rounded at the base and coming to a point at the top. This stone is worshipped as though it were sent from heaven. On it, there are some small projecting pieces and markings which people would like to believe are a rough picture of the sun because this is how they see them."[27]

---

[27] Herodian, *History of the Empire from the time of Marcus Aurelius,* V.5.

A depiction of his entrance into Rome

By all accounts, Elagabalus was deeply devoted to the worship of the Sun God and rose each day at dawn to sacrifice cattle and sheep at the temple he had built to honor his preferred deity. Senators were expected to attend these sacrifices and watch as "the entrails of the sacrificial victims and spices were carried in golden bowls, not on the heads of household servants or lower class people but by military prefects and important officials wearing long tunics in the Phoenician style down to their feet, with long sleeves and a single purple stripe in the middle."[28]

At each summer solstice, Elagabalus instituted a new festival in honor of himself (he was initially conflated with Sol Invictus) and was very popular with the masses as large quantities of food were distributed to all in attendance. During this festival, the black rock brought from Emesa was decorated, placed on a chariot, and paraded through the streets of Rome. Herodian explained, "A six horse chariot carried the divinity, the horses huge and flawlessly white with expensive gold fittings and rich ornaments. No one held the reins and no one rode in the chariot, the vehicle was escorted as if the god himself were the charioteer. Elagabalus ran backward in front of the chariot facing the god."[29]

Romans were used to the introduction and assimilation of new cults, and if Elagabalus had been less overt in his attempts to promote his god at the expense of the traditional Roman pantheon, he might have had more success in gaining acceptance of the Sun God as a form of Sol Invictus. As an apparent true believer, however, he wanted much more than that – he was determined that Elagabalus would become the chief god of the empire, taking precedence over Jupiter.

---

[28] Herodian, *History of the Empire from the time of Marcus Aurelius,* V.5.
[29] Herodian, *History of the Empire from the time of Marcus Aurelius,* V.6.

The issue came to a head in 220 when Elagabalus decided that his god needed one of the Roman gods as a wife. He chose Pallas, whose statue was kept in the Temple of Vesta, and he married one of the Vestal Virgins as a part of this scheme, but the plan so scandalized the Romans that he had to abandon his intention to move the statue. Not to be thwarted, Elagabalus replaced Pallas in his plans with Urania. He then had a huge temple constructed in the eastern style where the pair could be worshipped.

The emperor clearly aspired to change Roman religious beliefs into a monotheistic system, with the traditional Roman gods as mere attendants to the Sun God. Part of his program involved moving sacred objects from other religions to his new temple, and his actions alienated not only the Romans who worshipped the traditional gods but the followers of foreign religions as well, such as Jews and Christians, that he instructed to worship at his new temple. Elagabalus participated in the rituals of all of these religions, but that did not placate those who felt their religion was being slighted.

As if his efforts to elevate his god to preeminence in the empire were not enough, the emperor's sexual proclivities astounded and repelled a population that was far from prudish. As emperor, Elagabalus' sexual exploits appear to eclipse even those of Tiberius, Caligula, and Nero. He married three times (some sources say five) within three years and had numerous mistresses at the same time. As shocking as his promiscuity was, it was not his relationships with women that so disgusted Roman society but his relationships with men. At the time, homosexuality in Rome was not as acceptable as it had been in centuries past, and Elagabalus's particular brand was even less so. Elagabalus was, in modern terms, both a bisexual and cross-dresser. He was known to enjoy dressing up as a prostitute and would ply his trade in the bars and dives of the city.

Historia Augusta reveals that the young emperor was particularly obsessed with his appearance: "He would wear a tunic made wholly of cloth of gold, or one made of purple, or a Persian one studded with jewels and at such times he would say that he felt oppressed by the weight of his pleasures. He even wore jewels on his shoes sometimes engraved ones, a practice which aroused the derision of all, as if forsooth, the engraving of famous artists could be seen on jewels attached to his feet. He wished to wear also a jewelled diadem in order that his beauty might be increased and his face look more like a woman's and in his own house he did wear one."[30]

The emperor's excesses culminated in his "marriage" to a slave named Hierocles who, as the emperor's husband, was permitted to beat him. Not content with looking and acting like a woman, Elagabalus wanted to become one physically, and he asked doctors to carry out a sex change operation on him. When they pleaded a lack of ability, he tried it himself but failed and ended up having himself circumcised instead. He became notorious for using officials to search

---

[30] *Historia Augusta*, 'Life of Elagabalus', XXIII.

out men of whatever rank who were particularly well-endowed and force them to engage in sexual activities with him.

The esteemed Roman historian Edward Gibbon vividly described the emperor's shocking behavior: "To confound the order of the season and climate, to sport with the passions and prejudices of his subjects, and to subvert every law of nature and decency, were in the number of his most delicious amusements. A long train of concubines, and a rapid succession of wives, among whom was a vestal virgin, ravished by force from her sacred asylum, were insufficient to satisfy the impotence of his passions. The master of the Roman world affected to copy the manners and dress of the female sex, preferring the distaff to the sceptre, and dishonored the principal dignities of the empire by distributing them among his numerous lovers; one of whom was publicly invested with the title and authority of the emperor's, or, as he more properly styled himself, the empress's husband. It may seem probable, the vices and follies of Elagabalus have been adorned by fancy, and blackened by prejudice. Yet, confining ourselves to the public scenes displayed before the Roman people, and attested by grave and contemporary historians, their inexpressible infamy surpasses that of any other age or country."

This horrified the Roman aristocracy, but they were even more upset with the emperor's practice of promoting those to positions of authority within the empire from the lowest of classes. One notable example was the appointment of Publius Valerius Comazon, the son of a dancer and an actor, as commander of the Praetorian Guard in 218.

Unsurprisingly, the army, upon which he relied, eventually tired of his escapades. There were several failed mutinies before 221. when the emperor's family persuaded him to adopt his cousin, Bassianus Alexianus (known later as Alexander Severus), as his heir. They hoped that through such an action, the army might be placated and Elagabalus's reign could be saved, but Alexander's elevation led to a direct contest between the two for power within the empire. Elagabalus tried to have his cousin murdered in 221, but no one would carry out his order. The emperor tried again in March 222 when he visited the Praetorian Guard camp and ordered them to kill Alexander. They assassinated him instead, reportedly in the latrine where he had hidden. His mother was murdered at the same time. Both of their bodies were beheaded, dragged naked through the streets, and thrown into the Tiber, a traditional punishment for criminals.

Elagabalus reigned for less than three years, but given his behavior, it is perhaps more surprising that he lasted even that long. His youth may have protected him to an extent - he was still only 18 when he was murdered – but the real reason is that the important women in his life were able to manage his affairs of state effectively. It was only when Julia Maesa and Julia Soaemias fell out and supported different rivals for the throne that the wheels truly came off for Elagabalus. Without their combined efforts mitigating his excesses, the prognosis for the empire became dire.

Alexander Severus

Alexander Severus

While opinions of Elagabalus could hardly be more damning, history's judgment of Alexander Severus has been extremely positive. According to historian Aurelius Victor, "Although he held power no more than thirteen years he left the state strengthened on every side. From Romulus to Septimius the state had grown steadily in power but it reached its apogee under the government of Caracalla. It was due to Alexander that it did not immediately decline."[31] The assessment by ancient historians was that Alexander was a model emperor, and they pointed to the stability he brought to the empire after Elagabalus's reign as proof of his abilities.

Despite the praise heaped on him, however, many modern historians have questioned the almost universal reverence in which Alexander was held. Many point out that the real power lay with his grandmother, the redoubtable Julia Maesa, and that things took a turn when she died in 224 with his mother, Julia Mamaea. Alexander came to resent what he deemed his mother's extravagance and her tendency to use her position to confiscate the wealth of those who crossed her, though he did nothing to restrain her. By 227, she had the title *Mater Augusti et castrorum et*

---

[31] Aurelius Victor, *Book of the Caesars*, XXIV.

senatus et patriae, or "Mother of the emperor, army, Senate, and homeland." Later, this title was replaced with the even grander *Mater universi generis humani*, "Mother of the whole human race." Herodian wrote of Julia Mamaea that she "completely dominated her son, who did exactly what she told him. This was the one thing for which he can be faulted that he obeyed his mother in matters of which he disapproved because he was over-mild and showed greater respect to her than he should have done."[32]

The rather ostentatious titles notwithstanding, Julia Mamaea was discreet in most of her dealings with the aristocracy and took pains to include Senators in the governance of the empire. She created a group of 16 senators to make up a council advising the emperor. She moved to quickly reverse religious changes initiated by Elagabalus by sending the infamous black stone back to Syria and converting the temple built by Elagabalus into a temple to honor Jupiter. She was particularly concerned ensuring her son did not indulge in the kind of debauchery that proved so instrumental in bringing about the downfall of his predecessor. There is no doubt that she wielded considerable influence during her son's reign, and she was even able to arrange for the exile of his wife, Sallustia Orbiana, and the execution of her father. The key, indirect result of her well-known influence was that those disgruntled by various policies blamed her rather than the emperor, which ensured Alexander's reputation was protected.

---

[32] Herodian, *History of the Empire from the time of Marcus Aurelius*, VI.1.

A bust of Julia Mamaea

There was another key figure alongside Julia Mamaea in Alexander's early days: Ulpian, a writer and a lawyer. His importance in the history of Rome lies not in his association with Julia Mamaea or the emperor, but in his brilliance as a jurist. He was born in Tyre and produced a prodigious number of treatises on the law in his lifetime, along with authoring over 300 books. His works became key components of the Code of Justinian, and among his most important works were *Ad Sabinum*, which consisted of 53 volumes on private law, and *Ad Dictum*, which featured 81 volumes focusing on the edicts of praetors. The most significant, however, was the *Regularum liber singularum*, which still exists today.

Ulpian was made commander of the Praetorian Guard, and a number of significant powers were delegated to him. He used his power to introduce successful reforms, but he never managed to control the Guard in the way that had been expected. The Praetorians at the time were almost a law unto themselves, and one confrontation between the Guard and the citizenry resulted in three days of vicious fighting. Ulpian met his end when the Praetorians refused to carry out his instructions to execute Julius Flavianus and Geminius Chrestus, two of their junior commanders. The infuriated guards chased Ulpian into the Imperial Palace and murdered him.

Alexander Severus was only 13 when he came to the throne and 26 when he died, but his reign of 13 years was the longest held by a sole emperor since Antoninus Pius (138-161). The sculptors who portrayed him as a boy, a youth, and a man emphasized his qualities of spirituality and calm. He is, for example, credited with saying, "You should never do unto others what you would not have done unto yourself."[33] Many images adopted a classical style that was designed to differentiate the new emperor from the old, and he is portrayed similarly to Augustus, who was regarded as the epitome of a Roman emperor.

However, an accurate assessment of this young emperor's true abilities is difficult because of the manipulation of power by the Syrian princesses who played such an important role in his life. He never experienced a period in which this influence was not in play, because his mother died at the same time as him. He seemed incapable of challenging his mother over anything, including his wife, whom he, by all accounts, adored. Instead, he simply acquiesced to his mother's decision that his wife should go.

Unrest simmered beneath the surface almost from the time he took the purple. In 229, Alexander encouraged Cassius Dio, consul for that year, to go abroad because he felt unable to guarantee his safety. At the same time, a lack of discipline characteristic of Praetorians in recent years began to spread to the legions guarding Rome's frontiers. Unfortunately, this lack of discipline occurred just as the Parthians - who were now subjugated under the Sassanid Persian Empire - reinvented themselves. In 224, Persian King Ardashir defeated his overlord, Parthian King Artabanus, and in 226 he was officially enthroned as Persian emperor. He was renamed Artaxerxes in an attempt to associate the new empire with the glorious Achaemenid Persian Empire of the 5th century BCE.

Artaxerxes turned his attention to recovering territory lost to the Romans by the Parthians in northern Mesopotamia. In 230, the Persians took the cities of Nisibis and Carrhae, overrunning the Roman province. Alexander had no alternative but to meet this challenge directly, and despite his total lack of military experience, he set out for Antioch in 231, collecting troops from the Danube frontier on his way. The unrest among the legions did not go away, however, and before he could turn his full attention to the Persians, he had to deal with a mutiny by Traiana Legion troops who proclaimed a new emperor. The putative usurper committed suicide and the revolt fizzled out, but it was far from an auspicious start to Alexander's eastern campaign.

The actual attack on the Persians did not begin until 232 as a consequence of the mutiny in Egypt. Alexander led his army to Palmyra and Hatra, while other forces were sent northward to

---

[33] Cassius Dio, *Roman History*, IX.

outflank the Persians through Armenia and northern Iran, as well as southward toward the Persian Gulf. The northern attack proved relatively successful, but Alexander's column achieved little. By failing to advance at an appropriate speed, his southern forces were left exposed to the full might of the Persian army. Alexander withdrew to Antioch at the end of the campaigning season, and both sides had suffered heavy losses, but nothing was resolved.

The lack of the expected overwhelming Roman success was debilitating in terms of morale, and Alexander was accused of cowardice for not having led his part of the invasion more aggressively. Although it was not the overt victory hoped for, the Persians made no further attempts to invade Roman territory for the remainder of Alexander's reign.

As with many of his predecessors, Alexander labeled his campaign a success, and he was awarded the usual triumph. However, not long after celebrating his victory, he received news that the Germans had crossed the Rhine on pontoon bridges at several points. Alexander was not in a position to deal with the new threat at that point, so he bought off the invaders with promises of money. While this tactic was quite sensible under the circumstances, it was not approved by the legions, for whom the bribery was further proof that Alexander was not up to the task of providing Rome with the military leadership they considered essential for an emperor. Herodian commented, "In their opinion Alexander showed no honorable intention to pursue the war and preferred a life of ease when he should have marched out to punish the Germans for their insolence."[34] This was on top of Alexander's already having tried to reduce the overall military expenditure and cap pay and victory bonuses. In protest, they decided to proclaim a new emperor, Gaius Julius Versus Maximinus, a Thracian by birth who had worked his way up through the ranks and was held in high esteem by the rank and file troops.

---

[34] Herodian, *History of the Empire from the time of Marcus Aurelius,* VI.

A bust of Maximinus Thrax

After the troops had proclaimed him emperor in March 235 in a stage-managed performance in which he pretended to be surprised at the troops' actions, Maximinus led his forces directly against Alexander, who was camped nearby. Alexander was given the news shortly before the rebels arrived. According to Herodian, Alexander "came rushing out of the imperial tent like a man possessed, weeping and trembling and raving against Maximinus for being unfaithful and ungrateful, recounting all the favors that had been showered upon him."[35]

The troops camped with him swore loyalty to Alexander, but when the rebels arrived the next morning, they deserted en masse. The end came quite abruptly for Alexander. Herodian wrote, "Trembling and terrified out of his wits Alexander just managed to get back to his tent. There the reports say he waited for his executioners clinging to his mother and weeping and blaming her for his misfortunes. Maximinus was hailed with the title of Augustus by the whole army and sent

---

[35] Herodian, *History of the Empire from the time of Marcus Aurelius,* VI.

a tribune with some centurions to kill Alexander. They burst into the tent and slaughtered the emperor, his mother and all thought to be his friends or favourites."[36] According to *Historia Augusta,* Alexander's body was returned to Rome and interred in a magnificent tomb. He was deified by the Senate in 238, and a college of priests known as the *Sodales Alexandrini* was founded to maintain his cult.

Historia Augusta described Alexander as "the best of emperors," but the facts of his reign suggest that such an assessment is puzzling at best and simply disingenuous at worst. He had no positive military attributes, and his attempts at campaigning did not result in glory for either himself or Rome. By all accounts, he was a pleasant and agreeable individual, but these are hardly the qualities associated with the successful leadership of an empire as complex and riven with intrigue as Rome. Still, he did reign for 13 years, during which he enjoyed some clear successes, as the *Historia Augusta* noted: "He restored the public works of former emperors and built many new ones himself, among them the bath which was called by his own name adjacent to what had been the Neronian and also the aqueduct which still has the name Alexandriana [sic]."[37]

Indeed, Alexander put a significant amount of energy into his restoration and enlargement projects, as well as new commissions. He was responsible for the repair of the Colosseum, which had been damaged by lightning in 217. Alexander also completed the enclosure around the Baths of Caracalla, and he built a Nymphaeum in his bath complex, the Thermae Alexandrinae. He imposed special taxes to pay for the upkeep of baths throughout the city, a project believed to have been dear to him. It is said that he even paid for lamps so the baths could remain open after dark.

The Severan Princesses

While being kind and personable on an individual level and achieving success in his building projects, his attributes and achievements seem quite "unremarkable," and hardly deserving of the epithet "the best of emperors". There is no doubt that he was well-regarded apart from the army, and the question needs to be asked as to why this was the case. As alluded to earlier, much of the real administrative work of the empire during his reign was actually in the hands of two very competent women, both of whom, in effect, secured Alexander's favorable reputation. As such, no real assessment of Alexander's reign can be made without reference to his grandmother and mother, who both played prominent parts in his reign and that of Elagabalus.

After Septimius's death, the women in his life became the real backbone of the Severan dynasty. Julia Domna, his second wife, was the first to demonstrate that a woman could follow in the footsteps of famous Roman matriarchs such as Livia and play key roles in the political life of

---

[36] Herodian, *History of the Empire from the time of Marcus Aurelius,* VI.9.
[37] *Historia Augusta,* ' Life of Alexander Severus', XXV.

the empire. She was born in Emesa, Syria, to a family of Arab descent. Her name in Arabic meant "black," and her ancestors were hereditary high priests of Elagabalus.

Unlike most imperial wives, she accompanied her husband on his military campaigns and stayed with him in camp. Like her husband, she also involved herself in numerous building projects and was generally well-respected. Her greatest period of influence was immediately after the death of her husband. She acted as the mediator between brothers Caracalla and Geta and set the scene for her sister, Julia Masaea, to take on her mantle within the empire.

Like her sister, Julia Masaea was born in Emesa. As well as being Caracalla and Geta's aunt, she was the mother of Julia Mamaea, whose son, Elagabalus, became emperor. Also like her sister, she was politically astute – indeed, she was well-known for her plots and schemes and was instrumental in the restoration of the Severan dynasty. While Elagabalus reigned, she exerted enormous influence over affairs of state and remained the power behind the throne during both his reign and that of Alexander's. It could be said that she dominated Roman politics for nearly two decades, and when she died in 223, both she and her sister were deified. Her major achievement was engineering the accession of Elagabalus, and it was she who declared him Caracalla's son by her daughter. Her death was a severe blow to her daughter, Julia Mamaea, who was left to manage Alexander Severus on her own.

Julia Mamaea's father was Marcus Julius Gessius Marcianus. Unlike her mother and aunt, she managed to avoid any hint of scandal throughout her life and was regarded as a model Roman matron. While praising the education she ensured her son received and ensuring he was not corrupted by Elagabalus's vices, contemporary historians criticize her for dominating her son. She served as regent for him in his early years and initially ruled effectively. Along with reversing the scandalous policies of the previous emperor, she accompanied her son on his military campaigns. Naturally, she was jealous of any woman with influence over her son and used her hold over him to have him remove his wife from Rome. One piece of information that is of particular interest is that she is known to have received instruction in Christianity from Origen, the leader of the Alexandrian Christians.[38]

All three of these remarkable women proved themselves adept at increasing their wealth, and their skills were put to good use in the governance of the empire. Despite not being a part of the traditional Roman aristocracy, they exerted a huge influence on the empire that, by and large, was for the good, and without their administrative abilities, it is difficult to see how the empire could have avoided a major existential crisis much earlier than it actually did.

The Severan princesses played a number of roles, and their willingness to take risks to secure their objectives is one of their defining characteristics. It was their identity as "imperial women" that is, however, most intriguing. It is generally accepted that Roman women had little

---

[38] P. 14, *The Emergence of Christianity* by C. Whyte (2007). Greenwood Press.

independence, and their legal rights can, at best, be described as limited. The view of Roman society was that the woman's place was most definitely in the home, while that of men was the public sphere. These three women did not conform to that stereotype, and they enjoyed a high level of autonomy and self-governance. Their skills lay in living up to the expected gender norms while defying them at the same time. They acted in ways that were at odds with traditionally accepted roles, but they managed to retain respect, for the most part, from the male Roman aristocracy and the majority of the population. Of course, the whole system was such that they had to exercise their power and influence behind the scenes and officially through the men with whom they were associated, but their skill in manipulating them and events cannot be overstated.

The Aftermath and Legacy of the Severan Dynasty

The Severan dynasty lasted for approximately 42 years, with the brief interlude of Macrinus's reign. Septimius expanded the empire's territory more than any emperor since Trajan about 100 years earlier. He was fortunate in the sense that he did not have to deal with any major, simultaneous attacks on the frontiers, but that lack of aggression against Rome may well have been due to his aggressive policies when it came to deterring potential enemies. Some historians have suggested that by weakening Parthia, he paved the way for the rise of the new Sassanid dynasty that took control of a new, revitalized Persian Empire and became highly problematic for later generations of Romans. The greatest tribute to the Severan dynasty, however, lies in the fact that the 50 years following the murder of Alexander Severus are generally seen as the lowest point in the history of the Roman Empire until its actual collapse.

The Severans following Caracalla introduced a new sense of order, but their reigns were characterized by a gradual, overarching decline in imperial authority. In many ways, Maximinus Thrax embodied the changes that had evolved with respect to the background of a Roman emperor. Most notably, he was a common soldier who had risen through the ranks due to his military abilities. As Aurelius Victor put it, "Gaius Iulius Maximinus[,] commander of Trebellica, was the first of the ordinary soldiers who though almost illiterate, seized power…with the votes of the legions."[39]

Maximinus Thrax's lack of an aristocratic background was unusual, but what was even more surprising was that, though he was a Roman citizen, he was also a foreigner, hence his nickname Thrax (meaning Thracian). The future emperor began his military career around 190 CE by joining an auxiliary unit, and by 232 CE, he was a senior officer in Severus Alexander's campaigns in Mesopotamia and Germany. Maximinus was named emperor by his troops in Mainz in 235 CE.

Thrace was not highly regarded by Romans at the time, and Maximinus was frequently referred to as a barbarian by contemporary writers, but his military acumen assured him the respect of the

---

[39] Aurelius Victor, *De Caesaribus,* 25.

soldiers under his command regardless of his personal background. Thus, despite the opposition of the class-bound Senate, he was able to secure a reluctant confirmation of his accession to the throne in the wake of Severus Alexander's assassination.

Maximinus remained, first and foremost, a soldier, so much so that he never visited Rome during his three-year reign. Instead, he remained with his troops, undertaking a series of expensive campaigns that were bitterly resented by the Senators largely funding his exploits.

Maximinus was the tallest man to ever rule rome. The *Historia Augusta* claimed he was 8 feet 6 inches tall,[40] tales of his physical prowess were numerous, and it was said that he could pull fully-laden carts unaided. The size of his feet was also legendary, and eventually the term "Maximinus' boot" became a popular way to describe tall people. Surviving busts of the emperor show him as a muscular man with the close-cropped hairstyle favored by the army. Without question, he was a very different type of person from the meditative, ascetic Severus Alexander.

A coin minted in 236 that depicts Maximinus

As the opposition from the Senate would suggest, Maximinus faced insurrection almost from the very beginning of his reign. Within weeks, a group of indignant Senators conspired with their supporters in the army to dislodge him. Maximinus had built a pontoon bridge across the Rhine to aid his plans for invasion, and the conspirators intended to allow him to cross into enemy territory before they would destroy the bridge and leave him stranded on the wrong side of the river. Ultimately, the plot was uncovered before being put into operation, and those involved were arrested and executed. The emperor did not bother with the formality of a trial, and his actions signaled the style of rule he intended to adopt. A plot led by Titus Quartinus quickly followed, but this, too, was swiftly and efficiently suppressed without judicial proceedings.

---

[40] *Historia* Augusta, 'Life of Maximinus', VI, 8.

After dealing with these conspiracies, Maximinus crossed the Rhine in the summer of 235 CE and spent the rest of the year campaigning. Once again, his bravery and involvement in the fighting won him the continued admiration of his troops, and the Senate awarded him the title of "Germanicus Maximus." He next turned his attention to the frontier along the Danube River, and over the following two years, he was absorbed fighting successful campaigns against the Dacians and Sarmatians.

Maximus clearly knew what he was doing, but no matter how successful his campaigns were, they were enormously expensive, and wealthier Romans became increasingly disgruntled at the financial burden they had to bear to provide the resources demanded by the emperor. Maximinus was also becoming increasingly unpopular in the provinces, due in no small part to his reliance on property confiscations and downright extortion to replenish his coffers. Taxing the rich was one thing, but taking from the poor was an altogether different matter, and when he took money intended to pay for the corn dole, he made a fatal error. By 238 CE, Maximinus was universally despised, with the exception of his loyal troops.

The end for the emperor came in Africa Proconsularis, where his fiscal procurator had been particularly assertive in his tax-gathering endeavors. Both the rich and the poor resented what they saw as extortion, and a group of young aristocrats took the lead in defying taxation demands by murdering the proconsul while he was assessing the tax due on the olive harvest. They then marched on Thysdrus, where Governor Marcus Antonius Gordianus Sempronianus was in residence, but rather than kill him, they proclaimed him emperor. Their choice was nearly 80 years old at the time, and he accepted the position with little option, marched to Carthage, and sent word to Rome that he had accepted his elevation to the purple. The Senate, who saw him as one of their own, was delighted to confirm him as Emperor Gordian I.

Gordian I

The acclaimed Roman historian Edward Gibbon described the chain of events in detail: "An iniquitous sentence had been pronounced against some opulent youths of [Africa], the execution of which would have stripped them of far the greater part of their patrimony. (…) A respite of three days, obtained with difficulty from the rapacious treasurer, was employed in collecting from their estates a great number of slaves and peasants blindly devoted to the commands of their lords and armed with the rustic weapons of clubs and axes. The leaders of the conspiracy, as they were admitted to the audience of the procurator, stabbed him with the daggers concealed under their garments, and, by the assistance of their tumultuary train, seized on the little town of Thysdrus, and erected the standard of rebellion against the sovereign of the Roman empire. (…) Gordianus, their proconsul, and the object of their choice [as emperor], refused, with unfeigned reluctance, the dangerous honour, and begged with tears that they should suffer him to terminate in peace a long and innocent life, without staining his feeble age with civil blood. Their menaces compelled him to accept the Imperial purple, his only refuge indeed against the jealous cruelty of Maximin (...)."

However, the ancient writer Herodian was not at all convinced by Gordian's apparent reluctance to take the throne. Conversely, he asserted, "Although Gordianus declined the offer on the grounds of his old age, he was actually ambitious for power and not reluctant to accept it, partly because he preferred to accept the future danger to the present one and partly because now being an extremely old man he did not find the prospect of a possible death while holding imperial power such a terrible thing."[41]

In *The Three Gordians,* Gordian I was described as "characteristically Roman. He was becoming grey, with an impressive face, more ruddy than fair. His face was fairly broad, his eyes, his countenance and his brow such as to command respect. He was somewhat stocky. In character, he was temperate and restrained; there is nothing that you can say he ever did passionately, immoderately or excessively."[42] He was extremely wealthy, and he is known to have been fond of literature. In fact, he wrote, in verse, an account of the lives of Antoninus Pius and Marcus Aurelius in no less than 30 volumes.

Gordian I had a relatively undistinguished political career up to the point of his elevation to the throne, but he had been governor of Britannia. Given his background, his old age, and his expected compliance, he was in many ways exactly the kind of candidate the Senate wanted, and they quickly sent word to the provinces to rally support for the new emperor and his 46-year-old son, known as Gordian II, upon whom they conferred the title of "Augustus."

Classical Numismatic Group's picture of a coin depicting Gordian II and celebrating his military accomplishments

---

[41] Herodian, *Roman History*, VII.5.
[42] *Historia* Augusta, 'The Three Gordians', VI.1.

Maximinus heard the news of Gordian I's elevation while camping near Belgrade and immediately began a march on Rome. Meanwhile, in Africa, Governor of Numidia Capellianus led his troops on Carthage, and in the ensuing fight in 238, the younger Gordian was killed. Upon hearing the news of his son's death, Gordian I committed suicide. Their joint reign had lasted all of 3 weeks, which was so short that there were no imperial busts made for either of them.

The deaths of Gordian I and Gordian II left the Senate in something of a quandary. The support for overthrowing Maximinus was clear, and this obviously placed the Senators in great danger, especially when their favored replacements were now dead. Maximinus was not renowned for his clemency, so naturally the Senators decided that they had to act before the Emperor could descend on Rome. They held a meeting at the Temple of Jupiter Optimus Maximus and elected Decius Caelius Calvinus Balbinus and Marcus Clodius Pupienus Maximus as joint emperors, presumably in an attempt to mirror the concept of joint consuls. Portraits and busts depict Pupienus as a dour military man with a long, rather gaunt face, sporting a full beard and close-cropped hair. Balbinus was portrayed as more relaxed, sometimes reclining with his wife.

As this all suggests, the decentralized nature of power in the Roman Empire, some of which could be found during the reign of the Severan dynasty, became an existential crisis in the mid-3rd century. The years 235-285 became known as the "Time of Chaos," or the "Imperial Crisis." The crisis wouldn't be fully resolved until the reign of Constantine the Great.

It is to the Severan dynasty's credit that the rulers maintained the empire more or less intact for as long as they did, but none of them were sufficiently astute to understand and rectify the inherent and increasing weaknesses of the Roman imperial system. As individual rulers, they achieved a degree of success in restoring existing monuments and building new ones, but the weaknesses displayed by each, from personal weakness to sexual depravity, helped to create an atmosphere in which the prestige of the throne was diminished in the end. The role of the Severan princesses in maintaining order in the empire is increasingly recognized, and it is probable that without their guiding hands, the tendency to extravagance that was a feature of all of the Severans might have weakened the empire even more quickly than it did.

Septimius and his successors were avid builders, and Dio criticized them for their extravagance and what he deemed their wastefulness.[43] All of them relied heavily on the army's support to stay in power, often having to resort to bribery to maintain their positions. One way of finding the money to continue to keep the troops on their side was through the repeated debasement of the coinage, and the policy had negative consequences for the empire's economy in the end. Following Alexander's death, inflation was chronic, and many found paying their taxes unbearable as a result. This led to many abandoning their properties and refusing to take on any office as the financial responsibilities were too great.

---

[43] Cassius Dio, *Roman* History, LXXVI.16.

On the other hand, under the Severan dynasty, the development of Roman law reached its peak, and the influence of provincials within the empire accelerated. Papinian, the greatest of all Roman lawyers, was a Praetorian prefect in this period, and with Ulpian and Paulus, they accounted for over half of the entries in Justinian's *Digest*. It has been argued that these three had more influence on posterity than any other Roman writers, including Virgil, Cicero, and Ovid, and their perspectives on law have shaped the European legal tradition to the present day. Papinian was born in Edessa and worked in his youth as a legal assistant to Marcus Aurelius' Praetorian prefects, becoming indispensable to them. By the time of Septimius Severus, he was widely respected, and this led to his promotion to commander of the Guard. However, he was also the preeminent legal expert in the emperor's court and accompanied him to Britannia, and for some reason Caracalla hated him and had him killed in 212. As a writer, Papinian was renowned for his exactness and fluidity of composition. He wrote innumerable books and treatises used with those of Ulpian by Justinian.

The third jurist that contributed so much to law, both in Rome and later, was Julius Paulus Prudentissimus, known simply as Paulus. Less is known of his life than the other two, but it is generally agreed that he was of Greek descent, born either in a town in Phoenicia or possibly Padua in Italy. The assertion that he was born in what was then known as Patavium is based on an inscription bearing his name found in that city.

Paulus had something of a checkered career, serving as a jurist under Septimius and Caracalla before being exiled by Elagabalus. He was recalled by Alexander Severus, and his mother, Julia Mamaea, appointed him to one of the 16 adviser posts she created to assist her son. He served as Praetorian prefect of the Praetorian Guard for seven years between 228 and 235. His career path was not dissimilar to that of Papianus, and he was finally given the honorific title of Prudentissimus in recognition of his caution when expressing political or legal opinions. The Roman jurist Herennius described him as the last of the great jurists, and his work was held in high esteem both during his lifetime and after. He wrote 319 legal works, many of which have survived intact. His particular strength lay in his analyses of other jurists' work, and his assessments covered a truly enormous range of legal areas. A sixth of the *Digest* consists of Paulus' work, attributing to him the first articulation of the presumption of innocence in Roman law, *Ei incumbit probation qui dicit non qui negat,* translated as "Proof lies on him who asserts not on him who denies."[44] These three jurists had a far-reaching impact on law throughout the world in their own time, and their influence in modern legal systems has to be seen as one of the achievements that came out of the Severan period.

The influence of provincials within the empire is also an overlooked facet of Severan rule. Some argue that the Severans were part of the trend toward the extension of power to provincials, while others see them as being instrumental in bringing it about. In Septimius' reign, for example, out of 76 of the most prominent figures within the empire whose origins can be

---

[44] *Digest of Justinian* edited by A. Watson (1982). Philadelphia University.

substantiated, 35 were African. There is no evidence that the Severans had a conscious policy of "provincialization," but during their reigns, there was a striking increase in the number of provincials holding procuratorships, equestrian posts in the army, and centurion's rank. Septimius disbanded the old Praetorian Guard, which had almost entirely been composed of Italians.

All of these developments foreshadowed what was to come in the years following the Severans, and their reigns can be seen as a period of transition, carrying on trends that had been established in previous centuries while also being a harbinger of more chaotic things to come. At the same time, it paved the way for the empires of Diocletian, Constantine, and their successors, assuring them of their significance in the history of the empire.

Online Resources

Other books about Rome by Charles River Editors

Other books about ancient history by Charles River Editors

Other books about the Severan Dynasty on Amazon

Further Reading

Ackermann, Marsha E.; Schroeder, Michael J.; Terry, Jancie J.; Lo Upshur, Jiu-Hwa; Whitters, Mark F. Encyclopedia of World History, Ackerman-Schroeder-Terry-Hwa Lo, 2008: Encyclopedia of World History. New York: Facts on File, 2008.

Adams, Geoff W. Marcus Aurelius in the Historia Augusta and Beyond. Lanham, MD: Lexington Books, 2013. ISBN 9780739176382.

An, Jiayao. "When Glass Was Treasured in China". Annette L. Juliano and Judith A. Lerner (eds), Nomads, Traders, and Holy Men Along China's Silk Road, 79–94. Turnhout, Belgium: Brepols Publishers, 2002. ISBN 9782503521787.

Astarita, Maria L. Avidio Cassio (in Italian). Rome: Edizione di Storia e Letteratura, 1983.

Ball, Warwick. Rome in the East: Transformation of an Empire, 2nd edition. London: Routledge, 2016. ISBN 9780415720786.

Barnes, Timothy D. "Hadrian and Lucius Verus". Journal of Roman Studies 57:1–2 (1967): 65–79. doi:10.2307/299345. JSTOR 299345.

Barnes, Timothy D. "Legislation Against the Christians". Journal of Roman Studies, Vol. 58 (1968): 32–50. doi:10.2307/299693. JSTOR 299693.

Barnes, Timothy D. "Some Persons in the Historia Augusta", Phoenix 26:2 (1972): 140–182. doi:10.2307/1087714. JSTOR 1087714.

Beard, Mary. "Was He Quite Ordinary?". London Review of Books 31:14, 23 July 2009.

Beckmann, Martin. Column of Marcus Aurelius. Oxford Classical Dictionary, 2015. doi:10.1093/acrefore/9780199381135.013.8058.

Benario, Herbert W. "Marcus Aurelius (A.D. 161-180)". Roman Emperors.

Birley, Anthony R. Marcus Aurelius: A Biography. London: Routledge, 1966, rev. 1987. ISBN 9781134695690.

Birley, Anthony R. "Hadrian to the Antonines". In The Cambridge Ancient History Volume XI: The High Empire, A.D. 70–192, edited by Alan Bowman, Peter Garnsey, and Dominic Rathbone, 132–94. Cambridge: Cambridge University Press, 2000. ISBN 9780521263351.

Bowman, John L. A Reference Guide to Stoicism. Bloomington, IN: Author House, 2014. ISBN 9781496900173.

Bury, John Bagnell. The Student's Roman Empire: A History of the Roman Empire from Its Foundation to the Death of Marcus Aurelius (27 B. C.--180 A. D.). New York: Harper, 1893.

Champlin, Edward. "The Chronology of Fronto". Journal of Roman Studies 64 (1974): 136–59. doi:10.2307/299265. JSTOR 299265.

Champlin, Edward. Fronto and Antonine Rome. Cambridge, MA: Harvard University Press, 1980. ISBN 9780674331778.

Collins, Desmond. Background to Archaeology: Britain in Its European Setting. Cambridge: Cambridge University Press Archive, 1973. GGKEY:XUFU58U7ESS.

De Crespigny, Rafe. A Biographical Dictionary of Later Han to the Three Kingdoms (23–220 AD). Boston: Brill, 2007. ISBN 9789047411840.

Duncan-Jones, Richard. Structure and Scale in the Roman Economy. Cambridge: Cambridge University Press, 1990. ISBN 9780521892896.

Equestrian Statue of Marcus Aurelius. Musei Capitolini.

Gagarin, Michael. The Oxford Encyclopedia of Ancient Greece and Rome, Volume 7. Oxford: Oxford University Press, 2010. ISBN 9780195170726.

Gibbon, Edward. History of the Decline and Fall of the Roman Empire – Volume 2.

Gilliam, J. F. "The Plague under Marcus Aurelius". American Journal of Philology 82.3 (1961): 225–251. doi:10.2307/292367. JSTOR 292367.

Grant, Michael. The Antonines: The Roman Empire in Transition. London: Routledge, 2016. ISBN 9781317972105.

Francesco Gnecchi, I medaglioni Romani, 3 Vols, Milan, 1912.

Grant, Michael. The Climax Of Rome. London: Orion, 2011. ISBN 9781780222769.

Furtak, Rick Anthony. "Marcus Aurelius: Kierkegaard's Use and Abuse of the Stoic Emperor". In Kierkegaard and the Roman World, edited by Jon Stewart, 69–74. Farnham, England: Ashgate Publishing, 2009. ISBN 9780754665540.

Hadot, Pierre. The Inner Citadel: The Meditations of Marcus Aurelius. Cambridge, MA: Harvard University Press, 1998. ISBN 9780674461710.

Haeser, Heinrich. Lehrbuch der Geschichte der Medicin und der epidemischen Krankenheiten III. 1875.

Hays, Gregory. Meditations. London: Weidenfeld & Nicolson, 2003. ISBN 9781842126752.

Kemezis, Adam M. Greek Narratives of the Roman Empire under the Severans: Cassius Dio, Philostratus and Herodian. Cambridge University Press, 2014. ISBN 9781107062726.

Kleiner, Fred S. Gardner's Art Throughout the Ages: the Western Perspective. Mason, OH: Cengage Learning, 2008. ISBN 9780495573555.

Le Bohec, Yann. The Imperial Roman Army. Routledge, 2013. ISBN 9781135955137.

Lendering, Jona. "Antoninus and Aelius". Livius.org.

Lendering, Jona. "Lucilla". Livius.org.

Lendering, Jona. "Marcus Aurelius". Livius.org.

Levick, Barbara M. Faustina I and II: Imperial Women of the Golden Age. New York: Oxford University Press, 2014. ISBN 9780199702176.

Mattingly, Harold; Sydenham, Edward A. The Roman Imperial Coinage, vol. III, Antoninus Pius to Commodus. London: Spink & Son, 1930.

Mark, Joshua. "Marcus Aurelius: Plato's Philosopher King". Ancient History Encyclopedia. 8 May 2018.

Mellor, Ronald, review of Edward Champlin's Fronto and Antonine Rome, American Journal of Philology 103:4 (1982).

Merrony, Mark. The Plight of Rome in the Fifth Century AD. London: Routledge, 2017. ISBN 9781351702782.

Millar, Fergus. The Roman Near East: 31 BC – AD 337. Cambridge, MA: Harvard University Press, 1993. ISBN 9780674778863.

McLynn, Frank. Marcus Aurelius: A Life. New York: Da Capo Press, 2009. ISBN 9780306819162.

McLynn, Frank. Marcus Aurelius: Warrior, Philosopher, Emperor. London: Bodley Head, 2009. ISBN 9780224072922. Online review.

Murphy, Verity. "Past pandemics that ravaged Europe". BBC News, 7 November 2005.

Plague in the Ancient World. http://people.loyno.edu.

Portrait of the Emperor Marcus Aurelius. The Walters Art Museum.

Pulleyblank, Edwin G.; Leslie, D. D.; Gardiner, K. H. J. "The Roman Empire as Known to Han China". Journal of the American Oriental Society, 1999. 119 (1). doi:10.2307/605541. JSTOR 605541.

Reed, J. Eugene. The Lives of the Roman Emperors and Their Associates from Julius Cæsar (B. C. 100) to Agustulus (A. D. 476). Philadelphia, PA: Gebbie & Company, 1883.

"Roman Currency of the Principate". Tulane.edu. Archived 10 February 2001.

Stephens, William O. Marcus Aurelius: A Guide for the Perplexed. London: Continuum, 2012. ISBN 9781441125613.

Stertz, Stephen A. "Marcus Aurelius as Ideal Emperor in Late-Antique Greek Thought". The Classical World 70:7 (1977): 433–39. doi:10.2307/4348712. JSTOR 4348712.

Syme, Ronald. "The Ummidii". Historia 17:1 (1968): 72–105. JSTOR 4435015.

Thinkers at War. Military History Monthly, published August 2014. This is the conclusion of Ian King's biography of Marcus Aurelius.

Van Ackeren, Marcel. A Companion to Marcus Aurelius. New York: Wiley, 2012. ISBN 9781118219829.

Weigel, Richard D. "Antoninus Pius (A.D. 138–161)". Roman Emperors.

Young, Gary K. Rome's Eastern Trade: International Commerce and Imperial Policy, 31 BC – AD 305. London: Routledge, 2001. ISBN 9781134547937.

Free Books by Charles River Editors

We have brand new titles available for free most days of the week. To see which of our titles are currently free, click on this link.

Discounted Books by Charles River Editors

We have titles at a discount price of just 99 cents everyday. To see which of our titles are currently 99 cents, click on this link.

Printed in Great Britain
by Amazon